CELEBRATING THE NAME HELEN

Celebrating the Name Helen

Walter the Educator

Silent King Books

SILENT KING BOOKS

SKB

Copyright © 2024 by Walter the Educator

All rights reserved. No part of this book may be reproduced in any manner whatsoever without written permission except in the case of brief quotations embodied in critical articles and reviews.

First Printing, 2024

Disclaimer
This book is a literary work; poems are not about specific persons, locations, situations, and/or circumstances unless mentioned in a historical context. This book is for entertainment and informational purposes only. The author and publisher offer this information without warranties expressed or implied. No matter the grounds, neither the author nor the publisher will be accountable for any losses, injuries, or other damages caused by the reader's use of this book. The use of this book acknowledges an understanding and acceptance of this disclaimer.

dedicated to everyone with the first name of Helen

HELEN

In the annals of time, there gleams a name,

HELEN

Helen, in whispers of ancient fame.

HELEN

A muse of yore, a beacon bright,

HELEN

Her tale weaves through history's flight.

HELEN

In realms of myth, her beauty sung,

HELEN

A face that launched a thousand tongues.

HELEN

With tresses spun of golden hue,

HELEN

She captured hearts, both old and new.

HELEN

From Homer's verse to modern day,

HELEN

Helen's aura refuses to sway.

HELEN

A figure wrought with love and strife,

HELEN

A symbol of passion, woven life.

HELEN

In every Helen, a story untold,

HELEN

A journey of courage, fierce and bold.

HELEN

From Troy's ramparts to distant shores,

HELEN

Her essence echoes, forevermore.

HELEN

In gardens of thought, her name resides,

HELEN

A blossom of intellect, where wisdom abides.

HELEN

For Helen's mind, a treasure trove,

HELEN

A font of knowledge, a beacon above.

HELEN

In halls of art, her name is sung,

HELEN

A melody sweet, by poets strung.

HELEN

With strokes of paint and quills of gold,

HELEN

Her spirit dances, forever bold.

HELEN

In echoes of laughter, in tears unshed,

HELEN

Helen's presence, a thread that's spread.

HELEN

Through joys and sorrows, she stands tall,

HELEN

A testament to humanity's call.

HELEN

In the silence of night, her name resounds,

HELEN

A whispered prayer, where solace is found.

HELEN

For Helen's grace, a guiding light,

HELEN

A constellation in the darkest night.

HELEN

So let us raise our voices high,

HELEN

In praise of Helen, ne'er to die.

HELEN

For in her name, we find our song,

HELEN

A melody timeless, forever strong.

HELEN

In every Helen, a universe unfurled,

HELEN

A tapestry woven, across the world.

HELEN

So let us cherish, let us proclaim,

HELEN

The name of Helen, forever aflame.

HELEN

ABOUT THE CREATOR

Walter the Educator is one of the pseudonyms for Walter Anderson. Formally educated in Chemistry, Business, and Education, he is an educator, an author, a diverse entrepreneur, and he is the son of a disabled war veteran. "Walter the Educator" shares his time between educating and creating. He holds interests and owns several creative projects that entertain, enlighten, enhance, and educate, hoping to inspire and motivate you.

> Follow, find new works, and stay up to date
> with Walter the Educator™
> at WaltertheEducator.com

www.ingramcontent.com/pod-product-compliance
Lightning Source LLC
LaVergne TN
LVHW010622070526
838199LV00063BA/5237